CUSTOM CARS

Motor Mania

by Matt Doeden

Photographs by Chuck Uranas

Chuck Uranas, consultant, automotive photographer, journalist, and author

Lerner Publications Company • Minneapolis

Text copyright © 2008 by Lerner Publishing Group, Inc.

Photographs copyright © 2008 by Chuck Vranas except where noted.

Lerner Publications Company
A division of Lerner Publishing Group, Inc.
241 First Avenue North
Minneapolis, MN 55401 U.S.A.

Website address: www.lernerbooks.com

Library of Congress Cataloging-in-Publication Data

Doeden, Matt.
    Custom cars / by Matt Doeden ; photography by Chuck Vranas.
       p.   cm. — (Motor mania)
    Includes bibliographical references and index.
    ISBN 978–0–8225–7289–3 (lib. bdg. : alk. paper)
    1. Automobiles—Customizing—Juvenile literature. I. Title.
  TL255.D58 2008
  629.22—dc22   2007008652

Manufactured in the United States of America
1 2 3 4 5 6 – DP – 14 13 12 10 09 0 8

Contents

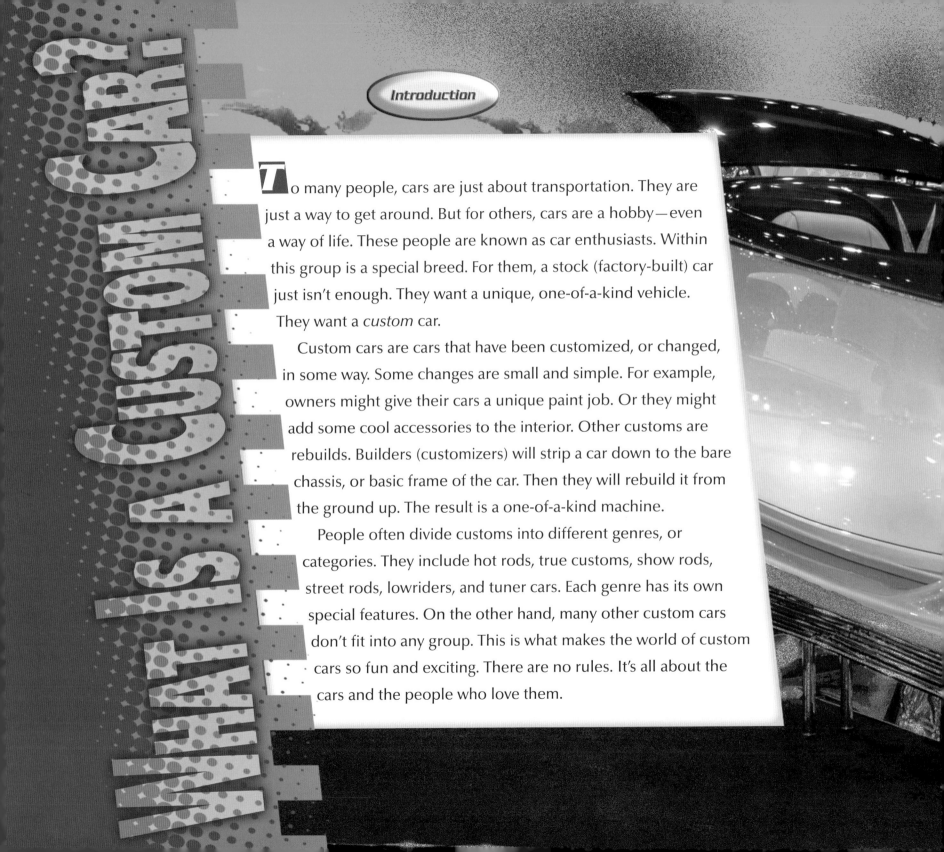

Introduction

To many people, cars are just about transportation. They are just a way to get around. But for others, cars are a hobby—even a way of life. These people are known as car enthusiasts. Within this group is a special breed. For them, a stock (factory-built) car just isn't enough. They want a unique, one-of-a-kind vehicle. They want a *custom* car.

Custom cars are cars that have been customized, or changed, in some way. Some changes are small and simple. For example, owners might give their cars a unique paint job. Or they might add some cool accessories to the interior. Other customs are rebuilds. Builders (customizers) will strip a car down to the bare chassis, or basic frame of the car. Then they will rebuild it from the ground up. The result is a one-of-a-kind machine.

People often divide customs into different genres, or categories. They include hot rods, true customs, show rods, street rods, lowriders, and tuner cars. Each genre has its own special features. On the other hand, many other custom cars don't fit into any group. This is what makes the world of custom cars so fun and exciting. There are no rules. It's all about the cars and the people who love them.

This customized '35 Ford roadster was an award winner at the 2006 Detroit Autorama show.

Chapter One

CUSTOM CAR HISTORY

Custom cars have been around as long as the automobile itself. In fact, the first cars ever built could be called custom cars.

Henry Ford proudly displays his very first working automobile, the quadricycle.

It all started in the late 1800s. No one person invented the automobile. Instead, many men worked separately. For example, Gottlieb Daimler in Germany and Henry Ford in the United States each followed their own ideas. They built their machines from the ground up. No two vehicles looked quite alike.

Those first cars were experiments. But they turned the idea of the car into something real. The next step was to design cars that were easy to build. More and more car manufacturers

appeared on the scene. Slowly, a system took shape. The carmakers designed a model of car. Then they manufactured new cars based on that model. The system was efficient. But each car was no longer one of a kind.

By the early 1900s, the demand for new cars was soaring. Carmakers looked for ways to build cars as quickly as possible. In 1913 Henry Ford's Ford Motor Company came up with the moving assembly line.

The idea was simple but brilliant. The workers assembled (put together) each car as it moved along the assembly line. Every worker on the line stood in a certain spot. Every worker had a single job, such as attaching a wheel. By the end of the line, the car was finished. The process was a huge time-saver. Within a few years, Ford was able to cut the time needed to build a Model T from more than 12 hours to just 90 minutes!

Ford Motor Company wasn't the first company to use an assembly line. But it perfected the process down to the last detail. These workers are at an early step in building a Model T.

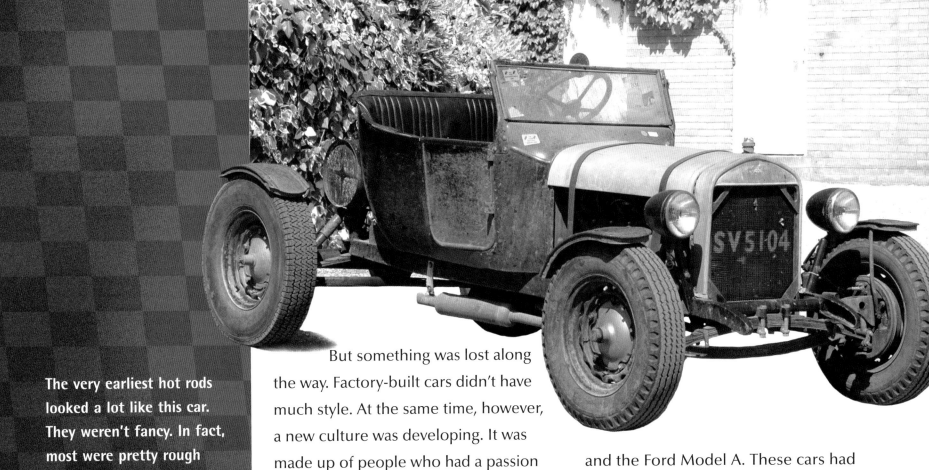

The very earliest hot rods looked a lot like this car. They weren't fancy. In fact, most were pretty rough looking. This car started as a basic 1924 Ford Model T. But the wheels, suspension (the set of parts that connect the wheels to the car), and front end have all been changed.

But something was lost along the way. Factory-built cars didn't have much style. At the same time, however, a new culture was developing. It was made up of people who had a passion for cars—and for speed.

Hot Rods

By the early 1930s, car racing had become a popular pastime in the United States. Most racers were young people. These were the pioneers of a culture that came to be known as hot-rodding.

Interestingly, the most popular hot-rodding cars were the Ford Model T and the Ford Model A. These cars had been built by the millions. They were tough, cheap, and easy to find.

Since racing is a competition, hot-rodders were always looking for a way to outrun their opponents. They "souped up" or "tuned" their cars' engines. Just a few adjustments or special "speed" parts added extra power and speed.

Meanwhile, a lighter car can accelerate (pick up speed) faster.

Henry Ford's Model T: The Ultimate Non-Custom Car

Henry Ford's focus on efficiency had its drawbacks. Every new Model T looked the same. *Exactly* the same. For many years, the car was only available in one color—black. Ford believed that offering different color options would only slow down the building process. But other carmakers realized that buyers wanted options. So they offered choices such as different colors, different engines, and different styles of interiors. They also updated their cars every few years to keep them fresh. Meanwhile, the Model T remained the same—for nearly 20 years!

Ford thought options were a waste of time and money. He believed the Model T was perfect. For years, he stubbornly refused to change it. But the public wanted fresh looks and new options. Model T sales began to dry up in the 1920s. Ford remained stubborn until the company almost collapsed. When he finally changed his mind, he produced another great car—the 1928 Ford Model A.

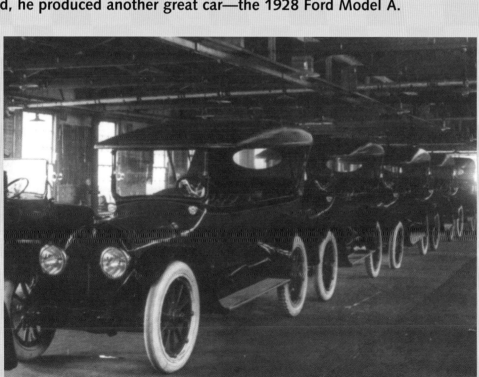

The 1932 Ford "Deuce" looked fast—and it was fast. This machine is a three-window coupe. The owner has chopped (lowered) the top and removed the fenders

So owners stripped the cars of parts they didn't need. They removed the fenders, windows, headlights—even seats! Looks didn't matter. The goal was acceleration, the thrill of speed, the joy of winning the race. These cars were the first hot rods. In a way, they were the first custom cars.

As the years passed, Ford remained the car of choice for most hot-rodders. The 1932 Ford was a favorite. Nicknamed the "Deuce" (*Deuce* is an old form of the word "two"), it had the perfect frame for building a hot rod.

The most popular 1932 models were the coupe and the roadster. The coupe was a two-door car with a roof. The roadster had no roof and no backseat. Without a heavy, metal top, the roadster was especially light. It was also sleek and aerodynamic—it cut through the air easily. When speed is the goal, every little detail helps. By the late-1940s, the hot rod-craze was at full speed.

Focusing on Looks

Meanwhile, a new kind of custom car—the lowrider—was appearing in the Mexican American barrios, or neighborhoods, of Southern California. Most young men in the barrios couldn't afford new cars or expensive engine parts. Instead, they bought inexpensive used cars. Big Chevrolets were a popular choice. But lowriders (as lowrider owners are called) shared something with hot-rodders. They wanted to drive something unique. So they focused on looks instead of speed.

For lowriders, "low and slow" was the goal. They liked how their big cars looked when they ran low to the ground. So they filled their cars' trunks with heavy bags of sand. The cars sat so low that they almost scraped the road. Lowriders also added fancy chrome bumpers and front grilles. Badges, sirens, bright wheel rims, and custom paint jobs soon became popular.

Then, in 1959, lowrider Ron Aguirre revolutionized the genre. He connected a system of hydraulics to the suspension of his car. The hydraulic system allowed him to raise and lower the body of the car. He could go low and slow just by pushing some buttons. Other lowriders soon copied Aguirre's idea. In the years that followed, no lowrider would be complete without hydraulics.

This beautiful 1950 Ford custom features an air-bag system that raises and lowers the body.

Coming Together

By the 1960s, customizing had become big business. A handful of builders had become famous for their amazing creations. They included the Barris brothers (George and Sam), Ed "Big Daddy" Roth, Bill Hines, Darryl Starbird, Gene Winfield, and many others. These creative thinkers weren't focused on speed like hot-rodders were. They weren't showing off their unique culture like lowriders did. Their goal was to build drop-dead beautiful cars. Their creations are what some people call "true" custom cars.

These star builders perfected several popular styles and techniques. They are still found on customs old and new.

For example, many of these classic styles are designed to make the car look lower, bigger, and tougher.

Sam Barris built this sweet ride for his own use. It's a 1950 Buick with many stylish touches. The front bumper was taken from a 1953 Lincoln. The front grille is from a 1953 Oldsmobile.

A chopped custom has had its roof lowered. A "chop job" gives the car a dramatic, sleek look. Channeling has the same effect. Channeling is lowering the body on the chassis so it sits closer to the ground. This is also called a body drop. Sectioning is cutting out a horizontal section of the body and then welding it back together. The result is a short, squat body.

The smooth look is also popular on customs. Shaving means giving the car an ultrasmooth look. A shaved car will have no door handles, badges, and other accessories. Frenching, or tunneling, means to set the headlights, taillights, and antenna into the body of the car. It creates a very clean look. Builders may also round off a car's corners, remove the bumpers, or add a few inches to the trunk or hood.

The final step in creating customs is usually the paint job. Builders like Gene Winfield experimented with eye-catching colors and styles. A candy apple paint job has many layers of shiny clear coat. A pearl paint job has a pearl-like sheen. Flames, pinstripes, and scallops were some of the most popular decorations.

This 1959 Cadillac *(above)* features the "fade job" paint style made famous by Gene Winfield. The colors fade together to create an eye-catching look.

Ed "Big Daddy" Roth

One of the greatest builders of the 1960s was Ed "Big Daddy" Roth (1932–2001). In 1959 he used a new material called fiberglass to create a car body from scratch. The result was a wild-looking roadster he called the *Outlaw*. The daring design earned Roth national fame.

In 1960 Roth opened his own custom shop. For the next several years, he built one famous custom after the next. His most famous car is probably *Beatnik Bandit* (1960). It features a clear bubble canopy (windshield), a flashy paint job, and a joystick-controlled steering system.

Custom Car Visual Guide

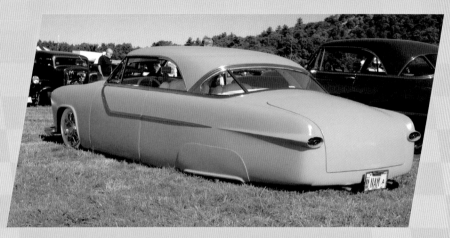

Channeled: body has been "dropped" to make the car lower.

Shaved: door handles and other details have been removed to give the car a smooth look.

Frenched: headlights, taillights, antennas, and other external parts have been inserted, or tunneled, into the body.

Chopped: roof has been removed and reattached at a lower position.

Flames: flamelike paint details have been added to give the car a "hot" look.

Scallops: lines and stripes make the car more colorful and eye-catching.

Pinstripes: thin lines, curves, and designs add decoration.

Sectioned: the body itself has been cut down and shortened by taking out a section.

The movie *American Graffiti* inspired one of the most popular TV shows of the 1970s—*Happy Days*. Both the movie and the show featured custom cars like those of the late 1950s and early 1960s. This custom hot rod appeared in the TV show.

The 1970s

In 1970 a group of car lovers formed the National Street Rod Association (NSRA). The organization is a way for car lovers to get together and enjoy their favorite pastime. That same year, the NSRA held a car show in Peoria, Illinois. The event was called the Street Rod Nationals. About 600 cars showed up. A year later, that number doubled. Since then the yearly event has continued to grow. The NSRA also holds a series of smaller events in cities around the United States.

The year 1973 was also a good year for custom cars. This was thanks to the hit movie *American Graffiti*. The film was created by George Lucas (who would later go on to bigger fame with his *Star Wars* series). Lucas based his film around the car and youth culture of the early 1960s. The movie featured many customs and hot rods. All the attention gave a boost to the custom car industry. Many new custom shops sprang up around the United States.

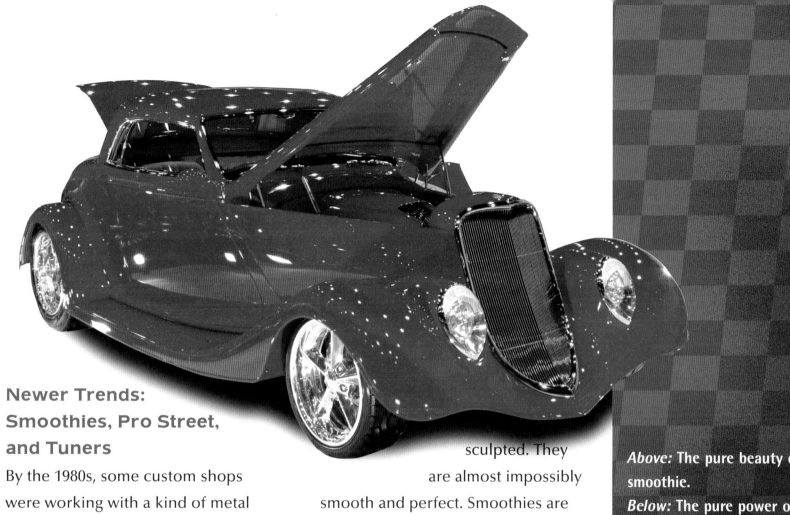

Newer Trends:
Smoothies, Pro Street,
and Tuners

By the 1980s, some custom shops were working with a kind of metal called billet aluminum. Billet is easy to work with. It allows builders to try many kinds of new looks. The "smoothie" (or "smoothy") is one of the most famous billet-based styles. Builders such as Chip Foose and Boyd Coddington perfected it. Smoothies have no visible hinges, body seams, door handles, or other features. Smoothies aren't shaved. They are sculpted. They are almost impossibly smooth and perfect. Smoothies are also very expensive.

The 1980s and 1990s also saw the rise of several new custom car genres. For example, pro street cars are beautiful customs with massive, powerful engines. Most are built from popular big-engined "muscle" cars of the 1960s and 1970s, such as Chevrolet Camaros, Pontiac GTOs, and Ford Mustangs. They feature roll cages,

Above: The pure beauty of a smoothie.
Below: The pure power of a pro street car.

This tuner car's interior is totally high-tech. Tuners are all about what's modern, new, and cool.

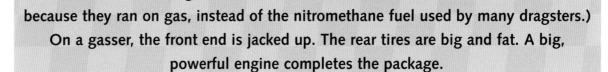

Gassers

While some car lovers look forward, others have an eye on the past. Gassers are a genre based on an old kind of car. They are built to look and perform like a popular class of drag-racing cars from the 1960s. (Gassers got their name because they ran on gas, instead of the nitromethane fuel used by many dragsters.) On a gasser, the front end is jacked up. The rear tires are big and fat. A big, powerful engine completes the package.

lowered frames, "jacked-up" (raised) rear ends, and fat rear tires. Pro street cars look fast and go fast. They are pure brute force.

Tuner cars are built for speed too. But they are small, light, and nimble. Most tuners are Japanese sports cars, such as Hondas, Mitsubishis, Nissans, and Toyotas. The engines on these cars are small but high-tech. They are tuned for extra power.

Owners of these cars focus on aerodynamics. For example, most tuners have a spoiler below the front bumper. The spoiler controls the flow of air under and around the car. It creates downforce: it guides the air, pushing the front of the car onto the road. This lets the tires grip the road better. Wing-shaped rear spoilers work the same way. They keep the car's rear end glued to the road. All of this equipment makes tuners fun to drive. And they look cool too.

Under the Hood: Flatheads, Hemis, Small Blocks, and Big Blocks

Ford Flathead V8

A full custom job often means an engine change. Most custom car owners like the power of V8 engines. (A V8 has eight cylinders arranged in the shape of a *V*.) The most popular models are the Ford Flathead, the Chrysler Hemi, the Chevy small block, and the Chevy big block.

Ford introduced the Flathead V8 in 1932. Its power and simple design made it a favorite with hot-rodders. The Chrysler FirePower Hemi V8 first arrived in 1951. The legendary engine's nickname comes from the hemispherical (half-globe-shaped) design of its fuel-burning chambers. Chevrolet introduced the small-block V8 in 1955. Nicknamed the Hot One, it delivered a lot of power in a very small package. Three years later, Chevrolet unleashed the bigger, more powerful V8—the big block.

Chrysler FirePower Hemi V8

Chevy big block V8

Back to the Roots, into the Future

In the world of custom cars, nothing stands still. Styles change and grow. Trends come and go. This is what makes custom cars so fun. You never know what is coming next.

One of the most interesting trends of recent years is the "hardcore" hot rod, or "roots" rod. The trend is a reaction to the flashy, expensive smoothies. It is a return to hot-rodding's roots, or early years. Hardcore hot rods look like the old machines from the 1930s and 1940s. They are customized for speed only. And you won't see a glossy paint job on this kind of car. Most have just a simple coat of flat (dull) black or brown primer. Like the very first hot rods, they are simple, rough, dented— and even rusty!

Sometimes ugly can be beautiful. This rusty old hardcore hot rod sure isn't pretty. But it brings to mind the excitement of hot-rodding's early days.

Every new trend seems to attract more and more car lovers. And so the world of custom cars keeps on growing. In the 1990s, more than 14,000 cars appeared at the Street Rod Nationals each year. But no one expected the explosion of popularity that came in the 2000s.

In 2002 the Discovery Channel cable network launched a new show—*Monster Garage*. The program stars the amazing Jesse James. For each episode, James and his crew build a new custom vehicle. Sometimes it's a car. Sometimes it's a motorcycle. But whatever the project is, fans have tuned in to watch. They love seeing a beat-up old machine turned into a one-of-a-kind custom.

Monster Garage was an instant hit. Soon other networks came up with their own custom car shows. The Learning Channel's (TLC) *American Hot Rod* stars customizing legend Boyd Coddington. TLC's *Overhaulin'* brings to life the amazing ideas of

Chip Foose. The Speed cable network has *Unique Whips*. MTV has *Pimp My Ride*. These shows have attracted millions of fans. Thanks to TV, custom cars are more popular than ever before.

Auto design wizard Chip Foose puts the finishing touches on an *Overhaulin'* project.

By the Book

The NSRA has a specific definition of what it calls a street rod. A street rod must be based on a car that was manufactured in 1948 or earlier. It must have been modified or modernized in some way. For example, it could have an engine or transmission that was made after 1948. A street rod also must be drivable. It has to actually work as transportation.

Chapter Two

CUSTOM CAR CULTURE

Nearly every genre of custom car has its own unique culture, or way of life. This culture is reflected in style of dress, hairstyles, and choice of music.

Slicking back your hair and putting on 1950s-style clothes—it's all part of enjoying the car culture.

At car shows, hot-rodders and street rodders often dress in the styles of the 1950s. Men wear jeans, white T-shirts, and leather jackets. They slick back their hair in 1950s fashion. Sweaters, Capri pants, or big skirts are the choice of women. And of course, these folks love their 1950s rock and roll and country music.

The lowrider culture is another example. Many lowriders are Mexican Americans. They take pride in their Mexican American culture. Most enjoy Latin music. They show

their Catholic roots by wearing crucifixes around their necks. Many even have murals (paintings) on their cars featuring Jesus and other religious symbols.

For people who are into tuner cars, it's all about being cool and cutting edge. They dress in the latest styles.

Their high-powered car stereos boom with modern, high-energy music like hip-hop and hard rock.

The list of genres and cultures goes on and on. Each has its own style and identity. But they all have one thing in common. They are a way for people to share their passion for cars.

Custom car lovers have a strong sense of community, like these people at the 2006 Alter Boys Jalopy Jamboree held each year in Worcester, Massachusetts. After all, what's the point of having a nice custom car if you can't show it off to everyone?

This Oldsmobile convertible is in the later stages of its rebuild. Its builders have already done the chopping and channeling. What kind of paint job would you give to this machine?

Building a Custom Car

For many car lovers, it all starts in the garage. That's where they spend their spare time—working on their cars.

Building a custom car is a big project. It's hard, dirty work. But it's also a labor of love. For a builder, there is no better feeling than seeing your car transformed into a one-of-a-kind machine. And knowing you did it yourself is a huge source of pride.

The process starts with an idea and a car. Most car lovers have a favorite kind of car. Some have always liked the old-school look of the Ford Deuce or the 1957 Chevrolet Bel Air. Some like brand-new machines, such as the Cadillac Escalade sports utility vehicle (SUV) or the Dodge Charger sedan. Still others prefer unusual models, such as the Ford Edsel of the late-1950s. They know that a rare car will really stand out from the crowd.

It's easy enough to go to a dealership and buy a new car. But getting an older car can be a challenge. Some of the most popular ways to find a classic car is through auctions and trade magazines. Auctions are events where people bid to buy things. The process begins with a certain price. From there, bidders compete with one another. Each bid raises the price. For example, the bidding for a car might start at $31,000. The first bidder will bid that amount. Someone else will offer

$31,500. Another might go up to $32,000. And so on. The bidder who is willing to pay the most gets the car.

Trade magazines and websites are another way to find cars. Buyers can browse the listings to find the machine they want. Many magazines and sites specialize in certain kinds of cars, from classics to sports cars. Car shows are another great way to shop. These events bring car owners together in one big place. They give buyers and sellers a chance to meet face-to-face.

After buying the car, it's time to go to work. Usually, the first step is to make a plan. What parts of the car need to be repaired? What needs to be replaced? Where will I get the parts? What kind of parts can I afford? Experienced builders plan these details at the beginning. That way they know what they will need to do—and what they will need to spend.

In addition, many people create sketches and drawings of the finished car. Or they might have a skilled artist sketch their ideas out on paper. The sketching process gives the builder a chance to see how the finished car will look. Once the work begins, the sketches are like instructions. They keep the project on track.

Ben Hermance of Hermance Design created this drawing of the StarWagon *(below)*, a futuristic custom car built from a 1960 Ford Ranch Wagon *(left)*.

Get Naked

To get a new paint job to look perfect, you need to start at the bottom. That means sanding *(left)* and stripping all the old paint from the body. The end result is a beautiful bare metal, "naked" car *(below left and right).* After fixing any dents or bumps in the metal, the painter can dress up the body with whatever paint design the owner wants.

Taking It Out

After the hard work is completed, the custom car is ready to show off. It's time to start up the engine and hit the road. This is an exciting moment. It's a reward for all the time and effort. If the car really looks great, it will draw stares and questions from total strangers. Car owners love talking about their cars almost as much as driving them!

Of course, the best place to talk cars is at car shows. Thousands of these events take place every year throughout North America. Small, local shows may feature just a dozen or so cars. Others, like the NSRA Street Rod Nationals, are huge.

Cruisin' Ocean City, held in Ocean City, Maryland, attracts more than 3,000 registered customized cars each year.

Grand National Roadster Show

Often referred to as the Oakland Roadster Show, the Grand National Roadster Show is one of the most famous custom car events in the United States. Every year, builders from around the world come to Pomona, California, to show off their latest creations. The gorgeous new cars always mingle with great customs of the past. Each year the show's organizers choose one fantastic roadster to receive the most famous prize in customizing—the America's Most Beautiful Roadster Award.

Many different custom cars are displayed at the 2007 Grand National Roadster Show.

Detroit Autorama

In many ways, the city of Detroit, Michigan, is the capital of the car industry. The Big Three U.S. automakers—General Motors, Ford, and Chrysler—are all based in the Detroit area. So it makes sense that one of the world's biggest auto shows takes place there every year. The Autorama features show rods, street rods, classic machines from the past, and much more. The event's top prize is the Ridler Award. It goes to the best newly built custom car that has never before been shown.

The crowds at the Detroit Autorama in 2007

Shows host thousands of cars in many different genres. Tens of thousands of people gather to show off their cars and soak up the culture. Shows are the place to swap stories, pass along customizing tips, and see the latest styles and trends.

Competitions are a highlight of these events. Judges award trophies to the best machines. The cars are judged on style, quality of work, and many other factors. The competition can be fierce. The biggest shows, such as the Detroit Autorama in Detroit, Michigan, and the Grand National Roadster Show in Pomona, California, attract the world's top talents. Competitors spend huge amounts of time and money to take home the top prize.

In fact, the drive to win has created a split in the car culture. Some call it the show-versus-go debate. Most owners build their custom rides for driving. For these people, this is the whole point of customizing a car.

Mail Slot

Some hot-rodders like to chop their roofs so low that only a few inches of window remains (left). These windows are called mail slots because they look like the small openings of a mailbox.

Yet some people have different goals. They build cars just for show. When they're done, they load their "show rods" onto trailers. They never take them out onto the open road. The machines are just too expensive to risk damaging. In fact, some of these show rods don't even run. In some ways, these cars aren't truly vehicles. They are works of art. They are masterpieces of style and craftsmanship.

Car owners cruise in with their favorite rides as another car show is under way.

Custom Car Clubs

Clubs are another way to connect with the custom car community. In fact, most car shows are organized by clubs. These groups come in all sizes—large or small, local or international. A small club may just be a bunch of car lovers who get together once a month to hang out and talk cars. Larger groups, such as Kustom Kemps of America, have thousands of members and a national headquarters. (*Kemp* is an old slang term for an automobile.)

Most clubs focus on a certain genre of car. The larger groups have websites and produce magazines and newsletters. Some have chapters (smaller, local groups) around the country. Car clubs give people a way to share their favorite passion. And they also keep car culture alive and growing.

Pinstriping artist "Hotrod Jen" adds some fine lines to a Ford sedan.

Motor Media: Magazines and Websites

Before the days of television and the Internet, magazines were driving trends and customizing movements. They remain a powerful force in custom car culture.

Few magazines have had a bigger impact than *Hot Rod* magazine. Started in 1948, *Hot Rod* spread the culture of hot rodding around the country. In time, the magazine went on to cover many different genres. It paved the way for hundreds of other car magazines, such as *Street Rodder, Rod & Custom, Lowrider,* and many more.

Most of these publications have Internet websites. In fact, the Internet has allowed car lovers from around the world to communicate. Many websites include forums—online communities. Registered users keep in touch, sell parts, swap tips, and post photos of their creations. These sites are just one more way for car lovers to keep up with the ever-changing custom car scene.

Chuck Vranas' *Lady Luck II* is all hot rod. It might be lavender but don't ever call it ladylike! The car is so low in the front that it almost scrapes the ground. For loads of power, he dropped in a big-block Chevrolet V8 engine with almost 500 horsepower. This is one car that knows how to rumble!

1932 Ford Coupe

This Deuce is a classic street rod. It has a flamed paint job, whitewall tires, and a Flathead V8 under the hood. *Street Rodder* magazine built this car to celebrate the Deuce's 75th anniversary. It also served as the magazine's 2007 Road Tour Car. It led *Street Rodder*'s yearly cross country tour of North America.

The California Kid (1934 Ford Coupe)

Famous builder Pete Chapouris created this 1934 Ford coupe in the early 1970s. It went on to star in the popular 1974 made-for-TV movie, *The California Kid*. Pete's machine has a chopped roof, bright orange flames, and white pinstripes. Note how the car's doors open from front to back. These "suicide doors" look cool. But don't open them while the car is moving. You might get thrown onto the street!

Ford Model A Pickup

You won't find anything fancy on this Ford Model A pickup. And that's the point of hardcore hot rods. Steve and Ryan Kopchinski built their machine to look like the hot rods of the 1930s and 1940s. They gave it a channeled body, red rims, big whitewall tires, and a brown primer body. This rod's screaming Chevy small-block V8 is pretty hardcore too.

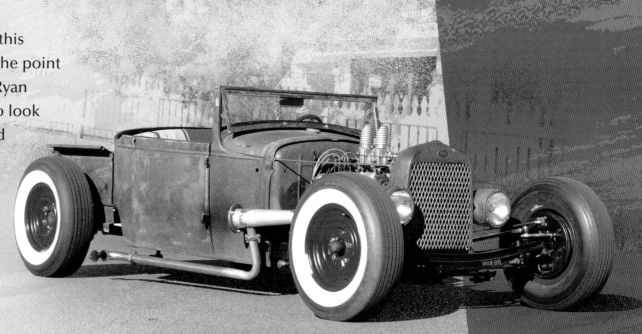

Scrap Iron II
(1935 Ford Pickup)

Scrap Iron II is another hardcore hot rod. Jim Derzius chopped the roof and channeled the body. Then he installed a 1938 Ford front grille. Chrome engine parts and pinstriping complete the classic "old-school" look. Derzius also added a roaring 1957 Chrysler FirePower Hemi V8 engine. This hot rod looks mean. And it sounds mean too!

The M-80 (1949 Chevrolet Business Coupe)

An M-80 is a big firecracker. And this car is pretty explosive. The crew at Hot Rods and Custom Stuff in Escondido, California, chopped, channeled, sectioned, and shaved this Chevy coupe. The M-80's one-of-a-kind front end has Mercedes-Benz headlights and a custom grille. This car won the Ridler Award at the 2001 Detroit Autorama for owner Chris Williams.

Cool Caddy Daddy (1951 Cadillac Coupe)

This car starred in a recent episode of Monster Garage. Jesse James teamed up with a gang of famous builders to create this smooth Cadillac custom. Darryl Starbird and Billy Gibbons were just two of the team's top-notch talents. They chopped, channeled, and frenched this machine from the ground up. Along the way, they replaced the suspension and added a fat Chevy big-block engine. And they did it all in five days!

Golden Sunrise (1958 Chrysler New Yorker)

The legendary Gene Winfield built this amazing machine in 1982. He chopped it, dropped it, and stretched the fenders. Then he added headlights from a 1972 Oldsmobile. The result is a sleek machine that looks fast even when it's standing still. The name *Golden Sunrise* comes from the car's stunning candy yellow paint job. Simple white scallops along the fenders complete the look.

Lu Lu's Passion (1958 Chevy Impala)

Gene Winfield is famous for his "fade-job" paint jobs. Check out the way he blended the colors on this car. This 1958 Impala's other true custom touches include a toothy chrome grille and a shaved body. Whitewall tires are a flashy touch. And this 1958 Impala's beauty isn't just skin deep. It has a king-size Chevy big-block engine under the hood. Owner William George named this beauty *Lu Lu's Passion*.

Beatnik (1955 Ford)

Gary "Chopit" Fioto needed four years to build the *Beatnik*. He started by removing the roof from a 1955 Ford coupe. Then he added a grille and bumper from a 1950s Cadillac. The gleaming chrome engine is a Chevy small-block V8. Custom-sculpted fenders cover the wheels. By the time he was done, Fioto had a jaw-dropping bubble-top masterpiece.

Mysterion (1963) Show Rods

Not everyone liked Ed "Big Daddy" Roth's show rods. But they sure got people's attention. *Mysterion* looks like a space alien's hot rod. Its bubble top, funky headlights, and candy-yellow paint job were all space age. Two thundering Ford engines give this show rod plenty of power. The car shown here is a copy of Roth's famous 1963 machine.

Road Agent (1964)

Road Agent is another Roth show rod. It looks like it was made for a science fiction movie. Copying race cars of the time, Big Daddy put the engine in the rear. This allowed him to try a really wild front-end design. The car's slim nose barely has room for the driver's legs and feet! Roth completed the car in 1964. It began appearing at shows in 1965.

Phaze II (1966)

Dave Puhl built this futuristic machine in the 1960s. Phaze II is not your average pickup truck. The smoothy body was made from scratch. And the engine design helped give the truck its shape. Puhl tucked the engine behind the driver. Then he gave Phaze II its ultralow front end. Will all pickup trucks look like this someday? Probably not. But it's fun to dream.

Hemisfear (2006)

Chip Foose's *Hemisfear* is half-smoothie, half-hot rod. The rear-mounted Chrysler Hemi engine delivers the power. The style comes from the perfectly smooth bodywork and brilliant green paint job. Foose designed the car's details on a computer. Metalcrafters of California brought the machine to life.

Magnitude (1940 Ford)

This 1940 Ford smoothie belongs to car collector Sam Magarino of New Jersey. The talented team at Lobeck's V8 Shop in Cleveland, Ohio, built it. *Magnitude* features a smooth body and a gleaming gold candy paint job. Chrome trim, engine parts, and rims add the perfect touch. Magarino's car is shown here at the 2007 Detroit Autorama.

P-32 Street Fighter
(1932 Ford Roadster)

Chip Foose's *P-32 Street Fighter* honors the U.S. fighter planes of World War II (1939–1945), such as the P-51 Mustang and the P-38 Lightning. (P is for "pursuit," and 32 stands for "1932.") Foose's fighter-plane touches include an aircraftlike interior and brushed metal bodywork. Under the hood is a massive V12 engine. This car may never leave the ground. But with that kind of power, it sure can fly!

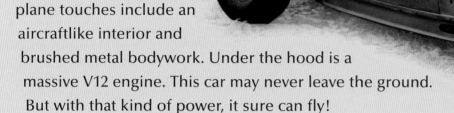

Impression (1936 Ford Roadster)

Chip Foose and his team built this beauty for owner Ken Reister. The job took more than seven years. But all that hard work earned them the 2005 Ridler Award, the 2006 America's Most Beautiful Roadster Award, and many other prizes. Based on a 1936 Ford roadster, the car includes more than 4,000 custom parts. Some people have said *Impression* is the most beautiful smoothie ever built.

1947 Pontiac Fastback

This car is an excellent example of a classic lowrider "bomb." The body's back end slopes down from the roof to the bumper. This style is called a fastback. Like many bombs, this car is loaded with cool accessories. They include a windshield visor, headlight visors, small wheels, whitewall tires, and fog lights. The tube mounted above the window is a "swamp cooler" air conditioner.

Latin Style 1964 Chevy Impala

Pete Salas's *Latin Style* is a perfect example of a lowrider "traditional." It features multicolored metal-flake paint and mirrored headlamps. *Latin Style* also has small rims and a wheel-hopping hydraulic system. Another lowrider touch is the stunning mural on the hood. And check out Pete's lowrider club plaque behind the back seat. Salas is the founder of Los Padrinos (the Godfathers) Lowrider Club of Saint Paul, Minnesota.

Impostor
(1941 Willys Coupe)

This 1941 Willys coupe is a pure gasser. The *Impostor* has a jacked-up front end and road-gripping rear tires. Note the "wheelie bars" sticking out behind the rear bumper. The bars keep the car from flipping over when it pops a wheelie off the starting line. The *Impostor* is owned by Mike Sappington of Ocean City, Maryland.

1965 Plymouth

Robert Schatz's 1965 Plymouth is one serious drag racer. Its Hemi engine delivers loads of power. And the car has an altered wheelbase. (The wheelbase is the distance between a car's front and rear axles.) Moving the axles forward puts more weight on the rear tires. This creates better traction at the starting line.

1968 Chevrolet Corvette Stingray

Look at all the chrome sticking out of this Corvette's hood. You know this machine has serious power. That's what pro street cars are all about. See the box with the black belt in front? That's a supercharger. It gives the engine a big power boost. On top is a high-tech nitrous oxide system (NOS). Nitrous is a powerful gas. A shot of nitrous gives an engine a power burst.

Nissan 350Z

This Nissan 350Z has every-thing a tuner could want. Its yellow-and-black paint scheme really stands out from the crowd. Wide wheel rims and thin tires are the favorite tuner style. Shaved bodywork and a custom interior add the per-fect touch. Under the hood is a fuel injected engine with an NOS.

Garson/D.A.D's Mercedes-Benz SL600

For most people, just having a beautiful Mercedes-Benz SL 600 roadster would be enough. But the Garson/D.A.D company makes products for people who want more. They created this ultimate "blingmobile" in 2007. (*Bling* is a slang word for "jewelry.") It went on tour with *DUB* Magazine's 2007 Custom Auto Show. The car is covered with 300,000 crystals. It has to be seen to be believed.

2007 Cadillac Escalade

SUVs are the vehicles of choice for many people. They like the extra space and luxury of these big machines. Custom builders like them too. SUVs have plenty of room to add powerful stereo systems—and even flat screen TVs! This Cadillac Escalade has a feature that really catches the eye—"Lambo-style" front doors. The doors open like scissors, just like the doors on a Lamborghini sports car.

Glossary

aerodynamic: shaped so that air flows smoothly over, under, and around an object

builder: a person who creates custom cars

chop: to lower or shorten the roof of a car by cutting some of it away and attaching it at a lower height

chrome: a coating of a metallic substance called chromium. Chromium gives metal objects a shiny, new look.

customize: to change a vehicle's appearance

fender: a metal covering over the wheel of a car

hydraulics: a system of pumps that force fluid into cylinders to lift heavy objects

roadster: a two-seat car with no top and no side windows

transmission: the set of gears that transmit power from a car's engine to its wheels

Selected Bibliography

Bertilsson, Bo. *Classic Hot Rods*. Osceola, WI: MBI Publishing, 1999.

Genat, Robert. *Lowriders*. Saint Paul: Motorbooks International, 2003.

Taylor, Thom. *Hot Rod & Custom Chronicle*. Lincolnwood, IL: Publications International, 2006.

Further Reading

Abraham, Philip. *Cars*. New York: Children's Press, 2004.

Braun, Eric. *Hot Rods*. Minneapolis: Lerner Publications Company, 2007.

Doeden, Matt. *Crazy Cars*. Minneapolis: Lerner Publications Company, 2007.

____. *Lowriders*. Minneapolis: Lerner Publications Company, 2007.

Harman, Keith, and Chuck Vranas. *Great American Hot Rods*. Iola, WI: Krause Publications, 2006.

Zuehlke, Jeffrey. *Henry Ford*. Minneapolis: Lerner Publications Company, 2007.

Websites

Custom Car Magazine
http://www.customcarmag.com
The homepage of this international magazine includes featured customs, question-and-answer articles, cruising and show schedules, and much more.

Hot Rod
http://www.hotrod.com
The home of *Hot Rod* magazine features hot rods, street rods, rat rods, muscle cars, and much more. Car photos, how-to articles, and feature articles are among the page's highlights.

Kustoms Illustrated Magazine
http://www.kustomsillustrated.com
If you're into lead sleds, *Kustoms Illustrated* is for you. This site features an extensive gallery, links to dealer sites, information about the magazine, and more.

Mr. Gasser.com: Ed "Big Daddy" Roth
http://www.mrgasser.com
At this website, you can learn about famous customizer Ed "Big Daddy" Roth and see pictures of his great show cars.

The Ridler Award
http://www.autorama.com/casi/ridler_winners.htm
Visit this site to see photos of every Ridler Award winner.

Street Rodder Magazine
http://www.streetrodderweb.com
The home page of *Street Rodder* magazine is a haven for Street Rod fans. It includes news, photos, forums, and much more.

Index

About the Author

Matt Doeden is a freelance author and editor living in Minnesota. He's written more than 50 children's books, including dozens on cars and drivers. His other titles in the Motor Mania series include *Stock Cars*, *Crazy Cars*, *Lowriders*, and *Choppers*.

About the Photographer/Consultant

Chuck Vranas is a photographer, journalist, and author living in Braintree, Massachusetts. His writing and images appear regularly in numerous hot rod and custom publications including *Street Rodder*, *Classic Truck*, *Custom Car UK*, *Rolls & Pleats*, *Mag-Neto*, and *Hop-Up*. His photography is also featured in the books *Great American Hot Rods* and *Hot Rod 500* by Kevin Elliott.

Photo Acknowledgments

The additional images in this book are used with permission of: © Chrysler Corporation, p. 6 (background); © Culver Pictures, Inc./SuperStock, p. 6 (bottom); © Ford Motor Company, p. 7; Library of Congress pp. 9 both (LC-USZ62-111278, LC-USZ62-111278), 22 background (LC-USZ62-115973); AP Photo/Damian Dovarganes, p. 21; © Mike Key, p. 42 (top); © Pete Salas, Founder of Los Padrinos, p. 42 (bottom).

The custom cars featured in this book are owned by: Kevin and Karen Alstott, pp. 4–5; Phil Wells, p. 8; Keith Cornell, p. 10; Dave Greenfield, p. 11; Robert Sylvia, p. 14 (top left); Patrick Guthrie; p. 14 (bottom left); John Rano, p. 14 (top right); Robert Middleton, p. 14 (bottom right); Fred Pederson, p. 15 (top left); Lynn Smith, (bottom left); Eli English, p. 15 (top right); Lou Cinque, p. 15 (bottom right); James Bedard, p. 17 (top); Bob Lees, p. 18 (top); Brady Bentz, p. 20; Paul White, Extreme Rod and Custom of Portland, Maine, p. 24; Mike Murray, p. 25; Josh Ford, p. 26; Troy Ladd, p. 28 (right); John St. Germain, p. 30; Peter G. Harris, p. 31; Steve Ramsey, p. 36 (top); built by Fritz Schenck, cover.